Empowerment through Sales

A proven & simple formula to positively shape the world around you

$$E = mcs^2$$

Travis N. Jensen

CYFworld Press books may be ordered through booksellers or by visiting:

Choose Your Fate world
https://CYFworld.com
and
CYFworld Press
https://cyfworld.com/cyfworld-press-1

CYFworld Press
ISBN: **978-0-9996813-0-5**

Library of Congress Control Number: **2020904833**
CYFworld Press, Peoria, AZ

DEDICATION

This book is dedicated to those who face long-hours, fear, rejection, and ridicule to make a positive difference in the lives of people and in the world around them.

CONTENTS

ACKNOWLEDGMENTS

Thank you

Sophia Jensen, my wife, for the inspiring encouragement to put what I've learned into print and for sharing the passion for making a positive impact on people

Erin A. Jensen for your work editing and formatting this book into finished form, while being a life-long voice of support

Coach Dave "Hunna" Brown *(Ogden High Head Coach, Track),* who believed I could accomplish what I didn't think possible during a time I needed it most

Tony Allred *(Professor of Marketing, Weber State University),* who first opened my eyes to the wide-spread impact of sales and marketing in the world around us

David Brandt *(Xtra-mile Group)* for simplifying the way I look at inspirational leadership and sales

INTRODUCTION

"It is not the critic who counts, not the man who points out how the strong man stumbles, or where the doer of deeds could have done them better. The credit belongs to the man who is actually in the arena, whose face is marred by dust and sweat and blood, who strives valiantly...who knows great enthusiasms, the great devotions, who spends himself in a worthy cause, who at the best knows in the end the triumph of high achievement, and who at worst, if he fails, at least fails while daring greatly, so that his place shall never be with those cold and timid souls who neither know victory nor defeat."

--- Teddy Roosevelt

Many misperceptions surround the concept of sales. Some people desire to enter a sales profession because they perceive it as an easy way to make good money. Others have a strong alternative reaction, declaring "sales is not for me," while displaying an expression that highlights the gut-wrenching thought of having to do it. Both altering views represent a lack of understanding of what real sales is. Even many of those currently making a career within the sales profession lack an understanding of the difference between selling and manipulation, as well as the difference between coercing an action and providing something the customer wants, and in many cases, needs. The fact is that every life is impacted by sales. Each person is presented with selling opportunities that impacts our lives every day, both in being sold to and in having the opportunity to sell. Understanding and incorporating real sales places you in the arena of life.

Sales is the act of helping others live a better life. It is the creation of win-win outcomes that transforms our home, communities and profession, regardless of our place in society. Understanding and developing the right sales skills can and will positively transform the world around you.

1

Introducing **Empowered** Selling

Mission x Connection x Simple & Specific x Smother
▪▪▪

Just like Albert Einstein's breakthrough equation for Energy ($E=mc^2$) paved the way for nuclear power by altering our view of the incredible potential for stable mass, the formula for **Empowered** Selling ($E=mcs^2$) transforms the impact we have in the world run by sales. Like nuclear power, **Empowered** Selling is literally life changing.

When looking at traditional sales, we have all had experience with salespeople who are pushy, manipulative, and a suck of precious time that we don't have enough of. It makes sense why sales carries such a negative connotation. Most of us have been sold something that we don't need and that does not bring value to our lives. Even when we choose not to buy, the time wasted speaking to a salesperson about features and benefits of a product or service that has no relevance to our lives takes away the time we enjoy spending with family and friends, or in getting the work done that matters to us.

Sales does not have to be what many people consider sales to be today. Both the sales process and the sales transaction should improve the lives of those we interact with and our lives by fulfilling needs we both have. Traditional or formal sales transactions are just a small portion of the sales that take place around each one of us every single day. Sales takes place when we speak to our children, greet a neighbor, explain the reason why we were speeding to a police officer, determine family values with our significant other, train a dog, and the list goes on to an infinite number of daily interactions. Whether we want to admit it or not, every person is a salesperson. Sales is a part of every person's life and the world we all live in.

Regardless of how much natural talent you start with, each person can become effective and impactful at sales. This book will provide you with an understanding of the fact that how effective we are at sales, impacts our personal and professional lives, regardless of our individual profession or social and family situation. Implementing the concepts in this book will move you into the "effective at sales" category on a consistent basis, which will literally change your profession, personal interactions and confidence in creating meaningful impact. To truly understand this concept, first, it is important to define what sales should be, and specifically **Empowered** Selling ($E=mcs^2$).

Empowered Selling is the transfer of a product or concept with a clearly defined **mission** that is **relevant** (connection) to the group or individual receiving it, and that leads to **action** resulting in **mutually beneficial outcomes**.

The specific formula for **Empowered** Selling is $E=mcs^2$. **Mission** (m), includes the mission of the product or concept, the mission of the person selling, AND the mission of the person being sold to. What are the goals of each? What drives or motivates the seller? What drives or motivates the customer? All are important in bringing about mutually beneficial action.

Connection (c) relates to how the product or concept is relevant to the mission of the person or people being sold to by fulfilling an unmet need. In addition to connecting the dots of relevancy, the old adage of *"people don't care about how much you know, until they know how much you care"* is also a component of connection. Truly understanding your customer and making relevant personal and professional connections that the customer can relate to, increases sales success. In general, people are more open to buy from those who share common traits, interests, experiences, or beliefs. One thing I have learned from sitting next to all types of people throughout my travels both in and out of the United States is this; we all have much more in common than we think.

Simple and **specific** (s), makes the selling message concrete and memorable. A more simple and specific explanation results in greater impact. Exactly how will the person being sold to benefit? Exactly what does the customer need to do in order to receive that benefit? This concept means eliminating all unnecessary words and being very clear with relevant features, benefits, and actions required.

Smother (s) involves reinforcement, reminders, and supplementation with additional resources or knowledge needed to follow through with the desired mutually beneficial action and to create long-term sales relationships.

Beyond "traditional sales" situations, consider the following scenarios:

Parenting:

Helping a 6-year-old child understand why it is important to brush his teeth every night before bed to prevent cavities, toothache, uncomfortable dentist visits, and to maintain fresh breath, to the extent that the young child is moved to consistent action without parental micromanagement is **Empowered** Selling.

In contrast, a child who only brushes his teeth as a result of threats or micromanagement, without the child gaining real understanding of relevant benefits (connection) and without the consistent early reinforcement required (smother) to form that habit is not **Empowered** Selling. Once there is no longer micromanagement or the ability to follow-through on threats, the child is more likely to miss brushing his teeth. An example could be when your child spends the night at a friend's house.

Doctor's visit:

From the patient's perspective, selling is used to help the physician clearly understand that the trouble she has catching her breath and the fatigue she experiences with routine activity is much more than just being out of shape. When that physician is moved from just counseling her on diet and exercise to referring her to a specialist to rule out more serious conditions, that is **Empowered** Selling. The mutually beneficial component is that the patient receives the correct diagnosis and help for that condition, and the physician receives better patient outcome ratings with reduced patient hospitalizations.

Coach:

Moving a high school track athlete from words that are intended to motivate, but that fall flat, to words and actions that instill true belief in her ability to do more than she originally thought possible on the track is **Empowered** Selling. "I believe in you. You can do anything if you work hard" can fail to have the intended impact if the track athlete's internal dialogue counteracts those words with the self-sabotaging notion of, "I'll disappoint them anyways, so I won't try." What is the difference between the two? True relevance (**connection**) to what the athlete needs to hear and see, **simple and specific** measures of progress, and **smothering** to celebrate wins and reinforce the positive comments.

Each of the following chapters dives further into each component of **Empowered** Selling, with concrete examples of relevancy both in and outside of what many consider traditional sales scenarios. After each component is explained in depth, real and applicable tools are provided to empower you to immediately begin incorporating **Empowered** Selling into your daily life. Each chapter is followed by a summary of key concepts. Buckle up and get a fresh cup of coffee. What you're about to read can change your life!

Summary: Chapter 1

- Sales is a part of every person's life and the world we all live in. Everyone is a salesperson.
- Regardless of how much natural talent you start with, each person can become effective and impactful at sales.
- How effective we are at sales, impacts our personal and professional lives, regardless of our individual profession or social and family situation.
- Implementing the concepts in this book will move you into the "effective at sales" category on a consistent basis, which will literally change your profession, personal interactions and confidence in creating meaningful impact.
- **Empowered** Selling is the transfer of a product or concept with a clearly defined **mission** that is **relevant** (connection) to the group or individual receiving it, and that leads to **action** resulting in **mutually beneficial outcomes**.
- **Empowered** Selling = Mission x Connection x Simple & Specific x Smother ($E=mcs^2$).
- The mission of the salesperson and customer are both vital in creating a mutually beneficial transaction.
- The connection must be made on how the product, concept or service is relevant to the customer's goals or mission.
- Interpersonal connection increases sales success.
- A simple & specific message on exactly how the person being sold to will benefit and exactly what they need to do in order to receive that benefit is critical for greater sales impact.

- Reinforcement, reminders, and supplementation with additional resources or knowledge (smother) are important in pulling through sales and in creating long-term sales relationships.

2

Mission

$$E=mcs^2$$

■■■

Outdoor survival is an interest and hobby of mine. What has kept me so intrigued with the untamed wilderness is that there is no better place to experience and learn about life in its most raw form. The lessons that the sometimes harsh and unforgiving wilderness teach, if not applied correctly, are literally the difference between life and death.

Imagine finding yourself lost and alone in a remote forest. There are a few essential things you're going to need for long-term survival. At the top of the list is your mission to survive. Without even knowing how to make survival a reality, the internalization of this mission multiplies your likelihood of success.

A mission is deeper than a goal. A goal or objective is something you set out to accomplish to achieve your mission. The mission sets the guiding principle(s) that the goals are formulated and centered around.

Just as important as the mission itself, is the *why* behind the mission. Why is that your mission? Why do you want to survive? The *why* is the fuel that drives your underlying desire to achieve the mission and specific goals and objectives contributing to it.

A *why* that reaches beyond yourself is much more powerful and sustaining as the work to achieve the mission becomes difficult. A self-centered *why*, such as a desire to survive because of your fear of death, is less sustainable than a *why* focused on coming home to guide, love, and mentor your children, knowing that their life will be much more difficult without you. You will be willing to do more and push through greater hardships with a selfless *why* as your motivation.

In a pharmaceutical sales scenario, when the *why* behind the work done is primarily to surpass company goals to earn a larger bonus, it is less sustaining than a pharmaceutical sales person whose *why* is centered around saving lives through persistence in education. It does not mean that both financial gains and saving lives are not considered benefits to each sales person, but when the selfless *why* is established as the primary driving force, more will be accomplished and mutually beneficial impact will be sustained.

Take for example, a situation where an uncontrollable market dynamic, like a physician retiring, reduces prescriptions for a medication the pharmaceutical salesperson sells. The effort this pharmaceutical sales person puts forth will wane when he knows that there is little possibility that he will achieve the number of prescriptions required to obtain a significant bonus. In contrast, when the mission is saving lives and making a positive difference in the disease his medications treat, the effort put forth by the salesperson does not decrease. In fact, oftentimes, the urgency and focused action to create impact for this unmet need increases.

Establish your mission:

For a parent, what is your mission? For my wife and me, it is: *We will raise our children to be happy, empowered, self-sufficient individuals who are engaged in the pursuit of their dreams and in the lessons life teaches us along the way. They will do this without inferiority nor superiority to others around them, while being armed with the courage to act with integrity and to stand-up for what is right.* When we look at how we parent, our goals and actions should all be aligned with achieving that mission. We aren't perfect as parents. We never will be. If I'm honest, everything we do today is not fully aligned with that mission, but the more we re-center ourselves around that mission, the more consistently our actions become aligned with it and the closer we move towards achieving our mission.

In the rare-disease bio-pharmaceutical market, my team's mission was more simplistic. *We will transcend what has been done within the rare disease space to improve patient outcomes by MAKING IT PERSONAL!* Goals and actions are directed towards innovation and accomplishing more than has been done in the past.

Each goal and action should also be fully aligned with improving patient outcomes by placing ourselves in the shoes of patients or their families and friends.

For a school custodian supervisor, a mission to do what he has to do to make a dollar, sets an entirely different trajectory than a purpose centered around a clean and sterile environment to enable healthy and productive education for the future leaders of our society.

In the following quote, Oprah Winfrey speaks to the fact that internalizing her *why* has been the driving force for not just her tremendous worldly success, but also internal fulfillment, despite the ups and downs she had both personally and professionally. "I live from the inside out. Everything I have, I have because I let it be fueled by who I am and what I realize my contributions to the planet could be."

Take time to ask yourself, in your profession or role within society and family, is your mission centered around superficial accomplishments, without a *why* that transcends self, or is it centered around changing the world for the positive within the sphere of influence you have been granted?

In summary, your mission and the *why* behind it sets your trajectory for what you will accomplish. In an outdoor survival situation, with survival fully internalized as your mission, your actions become aligned to that mission. Actions are used to accomplish goals like obtaining clean water, shelter or food, which all help to obtain your mission of survival. With a *why* that reaches beyond yourself, your mission is more sustainable as hardships occur.

The Customer's Mission:

The mission and goals of customers are just as important as our own. Uncovering the mission and goals of those we sell to offer key insights that help to create true mutually beneficial selling situations. This allows us to connect the dots on how our product, service or concept helps them achieve their goals.

Knowing your customer's goals, such as, improving school math scores for an elementary school administrator, provides a starting point to establish value for fulfilling an unmet customer need. If my product is an automated program that saves an hour each day correcting tests and assignments for teachers, I can connect the dots on how the product I represent frees up more focused time for each teacher to spend on specific math needs, which helps the school achieve their goal. As I connect the dots for the customer, my product establishes relevant value.

Going one level deeper than goals and gaining a clear understanding of the mission of the elementary school, which may be to be ranked among the top 10 schools in the state on a consistent basis, opens up even more opportunity to create value. Instead of just helping with math scores, my product sets the school apart with state-of-the-art innovation that can be used for enhancing the curriculum for subjects beyond their most immediate math score needs.

Understanding the *why* adds an even deeper level to connect on emotionally. When I uncover that the *why* is to obtain additional state funding to establish the best educational foundation possible for the children within their community, providing students the tools needed for success in life, even more doors open for mutually beneficial selling relationships.

New goals, not yet considered by the customer, may emerge as the understanding of my product and the understanding of the driving force behind the school's mission are merged. Ingenuity can now be used to generate ideas to further the school's mission with even more relevant possibilities for the diverse application my product provides for this specific customer.

Many times, our customers haven't taken the time to really determine their mission. They are acting on emotion or out of habit. Our line of questioning can prompt customers to think more deeply about what they really do want to accomplish, which opens up greater selling opportunities, as well as personal and professional satisfaction for our customers. Asking the question, "why is that your goal?" or "why is that your mission" will prompt these in-depth discussions.

Practical Application:

1. **Personal Mission:** Set time aside for reflection to determine your personal mission. Consider the following questions:

   - What is most important to you? Why?
   - What would you be willing to give nearly anything to achieve? Why?
   - What brings the greatest joy in your life? Why?
   - What is your fundamental purpose?
   - What do you value most?
   - If there were no restrictions and you could achieve any one thing, what would that be?
   - When you feel most fulfilled, what are you doing?
   - Who has made the greatest impact on your life? Why was that person so significant?

   Write down your mission in life. Remember, your mission is deeper than a goal. Goals can and will change. Eliminate excessive language (verbiage) and narrow it down to the essence of your purpose in life. After putting your mission on paper, revisit what you wrote tomorrow. Does this really capture the essence of why you are here? If it does, this should be used as a guiding principle in everything you do. As your mission evolves or adapts, rewrite your mission to reflect your evolving core values. Visit https://CYFworld.com for more insight and tools on mission and core values.

2. **Professional/Social Mission:** Reflect on how that life mission correlates with a specific product or role you play in your professional, personal, or social environment. What is it you are bringing to your customers? How are you making their life better? The following questions can help you formulate your professional mission or the mission for a role you play in society.

- What do I do? *(both directly and indirectly)*
- How do I do it? *(What core values do I hold?)*
- Who are my direct customers? *(those directly buying the concept, product, or service)*
- Who are my indirect customers? *(the people that benefit as a result of my customer buying the concept, product, or service)*
- What value does my concept, product, or service bring to the person directly buying?
- What value does my concept, product, or service bring to non-buyers, as an indirect result from the customer buying?
- What is the fundamental purpose of your given profession, product or service?
- What is possible to accomplish within the sphere of influence your given profession or social standing provides?

- What is the best possible outcome of your customer buying the product, service or concept?

Write down your professional or social mission. Exactly what is your fundamental purpose in this role? Eliminate excess and narrow it down to the essence of your purpose.

3. **Your Why:** Contemplate your *why*. What is the fuel behind your life and professional or social mission? Why is achieving your mission so important? What are the values you use as guiding principles in what you do? What are you willing to hold on to, regardless of how hard the situation or obstacle becomes? What would you be willing to die for? Your *why* may be immediately apparent, but it also may take days, weeks, or even months to find exactly what that is. Consciously realizing your *why* will provide the fuel needed to accomplish your mission. For some, their *why* is to make sure that the hard work and sacrifices their single mother made to provide opportunity does not go to waste. For others, it is to give a voice to those who do not currently have one. Your *why* is personal and only you can determine what that is. Write down your *why* and the values you will use as guiding principles for how you do it.

Summary: Chapter 2

- A goal or objective is something you set out to accomplish, but your mission includes your purpose and the guiding principles that the goals or objectives are determined and centered around.

- Having a clear mission multiplies your likelihood of success.

- The *why* is a vital component of the mission. The *why* includes the fuel that drives your underlying desire to act in pursuit of your mission.

- A mission with a *why* that reaches beyond yourself is much more powerful and enduring than one that is centered around self.

- Having a selfless *why* does not mean that personal benefits are not important, but when the selfless *why* is established as the primary driving factor, more will be accomplished.

- The mission and goals of those we sell to offer key insights that help to create true mutually beneficial selling situations.

- The deeper the understanding of our customer's goals and mission, the greater the opportunity we have to bring value and to establish long-term selling relationships.

- Fundamental questions provide the starting point for determining your mission. Deeper contemplation and reflection is often required to determine your *why*, which is the critical motivation behind what you do.

- Asking your customer, "why is that your goal?" or "why is that your mission?" will prompt in-depth discussions on what your customer really wants to achieve.

3

Connection

$$E=mcs^2$$

■■■

In a survival setting, high on the list of essential needs is water. Water comprises at least 60% of our body and is the key element that connects our systems and keeps our body working as it should. Because of that fact, a person can only survive a few days without water before the essential organs within the body shut down completely. Like water in the body, connection is the element in **Empowered** Selling that carries the essential items from where they originate, to the place they are needed, and in a way that is relevant to the individual customer.

Delivering and repeating a message is marketing. Marketing alone is not individualized or tailored to what is most important to each individual customer. Marketing requires a broad reach or a universal solution to meet your customer's needs when the price of the product or price of incorporating a concept is low. Telemarketers, billboards and television commercials arc examples of a marketing message in action. Marketing is a numbers game. Social Media ads take marketing a step further by analyzing habits of the online user to increase the odds of reaching a person more likely to buy a specific product, but the concept of what makes marketing work remains the same. The greater the number of potential customers reached, the greater the probability of a sale.

When the cost to buy the product or concept goes up or the benefit is difficult for the customer to automatically realize, the impact of a broad marketing message goes down. When the price is higher than the perceived benefit, personalized connection becomes very important.

Connection brings in a personal component and adapts the marketing message to what is most important to our target customer. For example, the cost of reducing time browsing social media apps in order for a teenager to clean his room on a daily basis is usually too great a cost, despite his parents frequently saying that his room needs to be cleaned to demonstrate responsibility on his way to becoming an adult. Connecting his room being cleaned to what is most important to him, not what is most important to his parents, is what is needed to achieve lasting results.

Establishing expectations and following through on consequences work when the child relates not cleaning his room with the loss of phone privileges, when that peer-to-peer interaction is a key motivational driver. The cost of not cleaning his room becomes greater than the cost of cleaning his room. This may create habits that last into adulthood. On the other hand, it also may not when those consequences cannot be enforced.

When connection is taken a level deeper, real change occurs and life lessons are taught. How does cleaning his room daily teach skills, discipline, and responsibility that help him become a better leader on the baseball team? How does that increase his fulfillment with his sport and peer interactions?

The ability to effectively connect is a sought after skill in professional environments and employees are compensated for it. For example, the salary and bonus of rare-disease pharmaceutical sales professionals is much higher than the salary and bonus of a primary-care pharmaceutical sales professional. A large part of the income disparity is due to the knowledge gap many customers have when it comes to rare-disease, as compared to common primary-care medications for conditions like high blood pressure. This lack of routine knowledge for a rare-disease increases the effort and customer cost to change an established habit, which in turn increases the selling skills, and specifically connection, that is required to change a habit and complete a sale.

Physicians who are experts within a specific rare-disease and that do understand the nuances of the disorder are much fewer in number. This means that the customer base for a sales professional in the rare-disease market is much smaller. This fact requires the rare-disease sales professional to be more efficient in creating impact with a smaller customer base.

Rare-disease sales professionals have to be better able to connect the dots for someone who lacks disease knowledge, and these rare-disease sales professionals need to be more efficient in creating impact with someone who does. These skills bring in greater revenue for the organization, and as a result, a higher salary and bonus structure for the sales professional.

The professional and financial benefits stretch well beyond traditional sales to every position that involves interacting with others. The ability to connect effectively is a critical component of Emotional Intelligence. Emotional Intelligence is our ability to effectively communicate and interact with others, while having a strong awareness of ourselves and exhibiting the ability to effectively manage our emotions. Emotional Intelligence has been shown to be a greater predictor of success than IQ, education, and technical skills.

The connection Empowered Selling incorporates contains two components:

1. How the product or concept helps our customer accomplish what is most important to them, and
2. Personal connection, which builds trust and capitalizes on the fact that we like to interact with people who are like us and who demonstrate genuine positive interest in us as individuals.

In a nutshell, **Empowered** Selling is providing a solution to a relevant need that can be adapted to any audience. **Empowered** Selling is individualized. Connection is what makes this tailored and mutually beneficial solution possible. When the price is high or a knowledge gap exists, neglecting strong connection to what is important to the customer will not result in the purpose, product or service establishing any real footing with our customer, which results in poor sales results. Connection also includes personal connection. We buy from those we trust and who show genuine interest in us and care for us as individuals.

In order to identify what is most important to our customer, as a fundamental principle for connection, two key tactics need to be leveraged:

1. Observation, and
2. Open-ended questions

Observation:

When lost or stranded in the wilderness with a mission to survive, you must first slow down and diligently assess and observe the environment around you. What are your most urgent needs? What tools do you have with you? What resources do the forest, desert, or plain provide? With careful observation, you may not find exactly what you want, but you will find the answers to what you need.

After getting lost on a hike and stranded overnight, you may want a tent, a nice sleeping bag, and a large steak for dinner. That's not reality. With our target customer, we may want them to think and feel the way we do, but that's not reality. Our job as a salesperson is to slow down to assess and observe in order to uncover what is important to our customer and to identify what is preventing him or her from achieving their goals. What obstacles are getting in their way?

For a parent, observation might include paying attention to the following:

What does your child do in his free time?

What makes her eyes light up?

What appears to bring stress or cause him to shut down?

How does she react to praise?

How does he react to constructive criticism?

What toys does she actively display or play with?

What does he draw pictures of or write about when able to choose his own topic?

When questions are asked, do the answers appear to be authentic?

True observation requires you to be fully present, which means not rehearsing your sales pitch in your mind or balancing your attention between incoming texts and the conversation taking place. Active Learning, where you are present only to actively listen and learn from your customer, is an effective strategy to being in the moment. No selling takes place during Active Learning. When the pressure of having to figure out how to sell your customer is mentally taken off the table, you relax. When you relax, you hear, see, and learn at much deeper level.

Just as in the wilderness, observation can be the difference between success and failure in a professional and social environment. Tattoos, pictures on the wall, clothes worn, displayed diplomas, accents, vehicles, bumper stickers, affiliations, ethnicity, pictures, social media pictures and likes, reactions to what I say, and reactions to other people and different situations all tell us a bit about each person.

For example, before my initial visit to an important potential customer in the rare-disease pharmaceutical world, the public data found on a social media site provided a breakthrough personal connection. Uncovering that this physician liked the television show, *Dual Survivor*, provided an opportunity to connect on a personal level. Outdoor survival is a passion of mine. Neither of us would have known about that connection if I had not taken the time to observe that social media site, which made the interaction more enjoyable and fruitful for both of us. This increased the time I spent with my customer and increased my customer's reception to what I brought to help him achieve his goals.

In many settings, the actual items observed do not matter as much as the story behind what we have observed. A picture of a scenic ocean view may be where your customer had their honeymoon. A University of Arizona sweatshirt may be where your customer's child is studying film production. Fidget spinners on a desk may be for an autistic child. Pictures with famous people may demonstrate the desire for affiliation with others that are considered important to society and may demonstrate the desire to be considered an important person. Tattoos are one of my favorite observations to ask about because they are often personal and provide me a glimpse into what's inside a person and what this individual holds as important. But, in order to know the story behind what we have observed, we must first ask our customers, or ask those with close affiliation to them, about what we have observed.

Open-Ended Questions:

Open-ended questions require an answer beyond *yes* or *no*, which prompts your customer to provide a more detailed answer. Open-ended questions are a very important tool to uncover customer goals and barriers that are in the way of achieving those goals. A customer response to open-ended questions can be expanded further by following up with, "tell me more." Depending on the situation, open-ended questions could include:

- *Tell me about what you do.*
- *What are the primary goals you are looking to accomplish?*
- *Ideally, what would you like to achieve?*
- *What does success look like for you?*
- *What are the largest obstacles that you're encountering?*
- *What is the most difficult part of what you do?*

Answers received for each of these questions can be used to connect the relevance of our product, service or concept. How does our product, service, or concept better help our customers achieve their goals? How does our product, service or concept better help our customers overcome obstacles or reduce frustration? Simple and specific approaches in effectively making this connection are described in the next chapter.

Open-ended questions should continue to expand beyond uncovering the goals and obstacles our customers have. Uncovering personal details help us connect personally with our customers. People want to be significant. One of the most simple, yet impactful ways to connect with another person is to show genuine interest in them. Despite that truth, next time you are out in a social setting, pay attention to how many people lack that skill. It is not uncommon for me to ask others about their life, engage in a half-hour conversation, and not receive any questions about me or my life.

Take another non-typical sales situation like dating. Having spent the majority of my career teaching and training others to sell, when I was thrust into the dating environment after a long marriage and a difficult divorce, identifying if someone held the qualities I was interested in and then making a connection came easier than I thought it would. I literally remember thinking, 'wow, where was this skill in high school and college?' The secret had to do with what I had learned in sales.

I asked about her interests, desires, and perspective on things. I shared small bits of similarities and connections as I uncovered them, but then quickly turned the conversation back to her. I uncovered what I needed to know to make a decision on whether I wanted to spend more time with this person. Yet, in many situations, she professed to want to spend more time with me, despite not knowing much about me. What my date knew was that I was genuinely interested in what was important to her.

People like to share what is within them to someone who shows that they care. People often do not remember what is said, but they do remember how they feel when they are with you. Having someone demonstrate genuine interest in you feels good.

Put this concept into practice today. After showing genuine interest in others, pay attention to questions you receive about yourself. Take time to reflect about those you like to be around. I will bet that those you like being around tend to show the greatest genuine interest in your life. Be that person who shows genuine interest for others in your professional, family and social environments. This concept alone will transform your relationships. This concept is also a driving factor for the truth that sales occur more often when the customer speaks more than the sales person does.

Another concept highlighted by the dating example is that people want to buy from someone they can relate to. When I ask questions, I'm looking for common knowledge, common interests, similar experiences and background, or even topics that I know nothing about that intrigue me.

I often start with statements or open-ended questions similar to, "tell me about…" and follow up with "tell me more" to uncover the story, learn more about the individual, and move towards real connection. We all have a natural and innate desire for connection. This approach helps to find what that connection is.

The combination of observation and authentic inquiry helps to uncover gaps, goals, needs or opportunities to what means the most to our customer. When we connect our product, service, or concept to enhance or support these customer goals, win-win solutions are established.

Let's talk about a couple of examples on how uncovering what is important to your customer is relevant in various settings.

When speaking to children as a parent, what is most important to them? If the child loves sports and expresses a desire to be a professional ball player, that knowledge should be used to tie in the benefits of how something we would like them to do, like homework, relates and helps them progress towards that goal.

An office receptionist, who has a goal to create an inviting and personal atmosphere for the organization she represents, will use knowledge obtained from questions asked on prior customer visits to further enhance and personalize the experience for them. For example, "how did your daughter finish out her volleyball season?" or "tell me about your trip to Hawaii."

A nurse will relate the importance of diet, exercise, and taking the heart pill daily as a means to maintain the ability to play golf once a month, after seeing her patient's eyes light up when talking about his time on the golf course.

Open-ended questions or statements that request the customer to "tell me more," are key principals in connection. These tactics require a response beyond a mere yes or no and encourages the customer to elaborate on their answer. When done with genuine interest, connection occurs.

Receiving Answers:

When you receive the answer to a question, receive it without judgment. Receiving without judgment does not mean that you agree with what's said, but that you respect the fact that they have the right to their own opinion. You also respect that their life circumstance or experience in life is their own and may be different than yours.

Applying non-judgment means that you are not making verbal or non-verbal accusations about who they are as a person. For example, a grimace, shocked face, or negative tone in response to an answer received is a very quick way to shut down the customer you are speaking with. In contrast, exhibiting curiosity around an area you disagree with or don't understand by saying, "tell me more about that," is non-offensive, does not shut your customer down, and helps you better understand their perspective. Your goal is to find true win-win relationships. Judgment is not a part of that.

Be genuine and authentic. If you're going to ask a question, listen to the answer. That also means, if it is an ongoing customer relationship, take notes on information, perspective and insight relevant to your customer. Be genuine in your curiosity for the questions you ask. Whether it is a sales professional I'm coaching in the field or a non-profit organization looking for donations, the largest indicator of inauthenticity is when they do not wait for the customer to fully respond. As a customer, when this occurs, I mentally check-out and the sale is lost, unless the product is something I know will benefit me, regardless of the salesperson.

For me, the most annoying aspect of many traditional sales people is the fact that they aren't authentic. They just want the sale, regardless of whether or not it is the right thing for me. That IS NOT **Empowered** Selling. **Empowered** Selling moves sales back to what sales should be...a WIN-WIN situation and a true person-to-person connection.

Establishing a better personal connection:

Trust is fundamental in each quality relationship. When selling pharmaceuticals, there are many times when the medications I am selling are the best thing for the patient, or at worst, just as good as the competition. When that is the case, I can be honest, authentic and passionate about discussing and selling my pharmaceuticals. When another product is better for the patient or the provider, I will let the physician know. This has established credibility and trust that resulted in my customers calling to consult me, regardless of whether or not they felt my medication is the best fit for a specific patient. This has increased sales for the right patient type and increased loyalty to my products when my pharmaceuticals were as good or better than the competition.

People have a strong desire to be important in at least one area of their lives. People want to be recognized for what they have done well or accomplished. We should never withhold expressing what someone does well or withhold sharing what we like and admire about another person. These compliments can be as simple as appreciating their choice of clothes or be as robust as highlighting the positive impact an older brother had on his younger siblings through his example of working hard and demonstrating responsibility. If we look for good, even in some of the most difficult people we deal with, we'll find it. You will be amazed at how genuine positive acknowledgment changes the negative demeanor of a difficult person. Be the person who is liberal in expressing authentic appreciation.

People don't like being forced to change. People want to be in a position to realize and understand that a change is needed, and then to make the choice to change themselves. Establishing context and bringing light to a problem that gets in the way of our customer accomplishing what is most important to them, followed by asking a question similar to, "what do you feel the best solution is, taking all we've discussed into consideration?" makes the solution the idea of our customer, which creates more impactful and lasting change.

This concept is true for anything that impacts other people. Take team goals and standards for example. If goals and standards are just dictated by the team leader, the rest of the team is less engaged in following them than if they played a role in establishing these goals and standards themselves. This is true even when the goals and standards are the exact same in both scenarios. Always involve others in what impacts them. When those impacted are involved and their opinion is heard, acceptance of the final decision increases significantly. Acceptance is increased when others are involved even when the final decision is different than the thoughts and ideas they advocated for.

People do not want to feel stupid for what they have been doing wrong. Condemnation is one of the quickest ways to lose connection. Empathizing and acknowledging why someone has made the choices they have up until this point helps people feel understood and reasonable for the choices they have made. This prevents our customer from shutting down. Statements like, "if I had been in your shoes, I'm sure I would have made the same choices" increases our connection to that individual, which allows further dialogue that instigates change. Follow-up conversation may be similar to, "now that we know what we know now, what do you feel is the best course of action moving forward?"

We do not have to agree with actions or statements another person makes, but if we were in that person's shoes, with the same upbringing and the same emotional disposition, we would feel the same as they do in that moment. Sometimes it comes down to, would we rather be right or would we rather move past what is holding us back from making a greater positive difference in the lives of others and ourselves? We all hate to be told we're wrong and that we have made a mistake that someone in our position should have never made. Allow others to save face whenever possible.

Practical Application:

1. **Authentic Praise:** Look for something you like with a person you encounter today. This can be someone you know well, or someone you have never met. Acknowledge and compliment this individual. How did they react? How did this approach change the way they are with you? Commit to completing this exercise every day for 1 week. Write down the other people's reaction and what occurred as a result of the interaction in a journal each day.

2. **Personal Connection:** Consider what you know and what you don't know about someone you regularly interact with. This could include a spouse, children, or a colleague at work. Ask about something you would like to learn more about. If the answer is brief, follow-up with *tell me more.* Listen to the entire answer. Accept what is being said from the person you are speaking to without any judgment. How did they react? What do their non-verbal signs tell you? If you learn something that is important to this individual, write it down and commit to incorporating it into how you interact with this individual within 1 week. The list of topics and associated questions you can ask about are endless. A few examples to get you thinking are listed below. Visit https://CYFworld.com for more question suggestions used to increase connection.

   o Where did you grow up? What did you like about growing up there?

   o What did you do last weekend? Tell me more about that.

   o Who are the kids you like most at school? Tell me about what it is you like about them.

   o What is your favorite memory from childhood?

   o Tell me about your tattoo. What prompted you to get it?

   o If money were not an issue, what would you do?

- o If you could be anyone, who would that be and why?
- o If you had to describe yourself in three words, what would they be? Why are those the three words you chose?
- o What three words would you like others to describe you with? Why did you choose those three words?
- o What do you love doing while hanging out with friends. Tell me more about that.
- o Who has had the most significant impact on your life? Tell me more about that.
- o What are you passionate about?

3. **Establishing Relevancy:** Use open-ended questions to uncover the goals and obstacles for a professional or personal customer you interact with regularly. Use Active Learning, where you do not sell your product, service or concept. When the conversation is complete, write down how your product service or concept can help your customer achieve what is important to them by achieving goals or by reducing obstacles in their way. Examples of questions you may use during this interaction could include:

- o Tell me about what you do.
- o What are the primary goals you are looking to accomplish?

o   What are you trying to achieve?

o   What is the most difficult part of what you do?

o   What would you like to be doing 1, 3 or 5 years from now? What would you like to have accomplished during that time?

o   What is holding you back from reaching your goals?

o   If you could change or achieve anything, as it relates to your current goals, what would that look like?

Summary: Chapter 3

- The higher the perceived cost of buying a product or incorporating a concept, the more important individualized connection becomes.

- Connecting benefits that are most important to our customer, not that are most important to you, is a vital component of **Empowered** Selling.

- The two important components of connection include how the product or concept helps our customer accomplish what is most important to them, and personal connection, which incorporates the fact that we like to interact with people who are like us and who demonstrate genuine interest in our wellbeing. This develops trust.

- Observation and open-ended questions are two tools leveraged to determine what is most important to your target customer, which is essential to establish real connection.

- Observation will not always provide the answers you want, but it will provide the answers you need.

- True observation requires you to be fully present, which means not rehearsing your sales pitch in your mind or balancing your attention between incoming texts and the conversation taking place.

- Active Learning, where you are present only to actively listen and learn from your customer, is an effective strategy to being in the moment. No selling takes place during Active Learning.

- Ask relevant open-ended questions or statements requesting to "tell me more" to uncover interests, goals, struggles and perspective.

- People often do not remember what is said, but they do remember how they feel when they are with you. Showing genuine interest by asking open-ended questions increases personal connection.

- Direct answers received from customers are not always the real answer, which solidifies the value of observation.

- Receive answers without judgment.

- If you're going to ask a question, listen to the answer.

- The more the customer speaks, the greater the probability of a sale.

- Doing what is right is more important than closing a sale and is essential for long-term sales success and personal fulfillment.

- Be genuine when showing interest in your customer and in your desire to help them achieve their goals.

- People don't like to be forced to change. Help connect the dots that makes the sale their idea.

- Always involve others in the decision making process for things that impact them.

- Allow others to save face. Condemnation is the quickest way to lose connection.

- Authentic praise breaks down emotional walls and helps to build personal connection.

4

Simple & Specific

The Message and Closing the Sale

$$E=mcs^2$$

■■

Simple & Specific is sharing exactly what the customer needs to know without unnecessary detail that dilutes the core message. An example of Simple & Specific put into practice are presidential campaigns. There are a multitude of complexities when it comes to running the United States government, but what is it that's emphasized? What is it that gets the candidate elected? *Hope and Change! Make America Great Again!* Simple and specific platforms connect with audiences and move the masses to vote for what resonates most with them.

When candidates speak to specific subsets of the United States population, the simple and specific message that *Hope and Change* or *Make America Great Again* represent to that specific population is emphasized. *Student Debt Relief* may be a sub-platform emphasized to university students concerned with paying off the debt accumulated with the increase in cost for higher education. *More Jobs* may be a sub-platform for a city significantly impacted by a failing economy. The details behind each of these sub-platforms are simplified and boiled down to a handful of bullet-points. The philosophy for Simple & Specific is simple. Give the audience what they need, nothing more.

Let's take a look at the legal system in a divorce proceeding that involves a dispute over child custody. There are specific laws clearly defined that judges use to determine the ruling. A client may want her lawyer to bring up in court the lying and cheating that took place during her marriage. It feels good to vent and express the morally wrong things that have occurred, but infidelity and deceit, as it pertains to a spouse, does not have relevancy within the court of law on whether or not the father should lose his right to his children. A good lawyer will remain focused on reminding the court about legal precedent and how specific acts from the father constitute child abuse or neglect under the law. The more dialogue that distracts from those few facts, the more diluted and less impactful the message is.

There are complex issues that may require a lot of dialogue and explanation, but in each situation, the simple and specific summary points should be a focus at the beginning and at the end of the conversation. Let's look at selling a specialized luxury car. There will be in-depth features important to highlight to the customer who is considering paying a small fortune for this automobile, but the initial core selling message may be something similar to the following:

"The X series Zenith Sports Coup provides unmatched performance, coupled with ultimate luxury that stands apart from any other vehicle on the road."

This core selling message takes into consideration what is important to the customer and is followed by the simple and specific detail required to support those claims. After completing a more detailed explanation of what is important for the customer to know, a summary statement is used to reinforce those key points in a simple and specific manner, like stated below:

"Taking into consideration the performance that was important to you, the luxury feel you said you would like to have, and the fact that this vehicle makes a statement like no other vehicle on the road, how do you feel about getting behind the wheel?"

As I teach people this concept, I ask them to boil down the core selling message of *why this product*, to a 30 second or less soundbite. A longer explanation of features and benefits upfront dilutes the impact of the core message. It dilutes the message of what they need to know. Your tailored soundbite hooks your audience and gives them a reason to listen. The summary simplifies everything discussed into the raw key attributes that the customer needs to know, from their perspective, to make a decision.

For another customer, the soundbite could be very different for the exact same product. What if open-ended questions uncovered that luxury is important for the customer personally, but safety is an even higher priority for him, knowing that his 17-year-old daughter will be driving the car on occasion? The core selling message may look like this: *"The X series Zenith Sports Coup provides unmatched performance and luxury, with one of the highest safety ratings of any car in its class."*

When formulating simple and specific core selling messages, differentiating language is an important component. Words like *only, best, highest, most, unmatched,* and *like no other* highlight the areas that make your product distinctly different from the competition. Without differentiating language, messages from competing products often sound the same, which lessens your impact and decreases positive sales results.

Statement of Fact + Open-ended Question

People who love to talk make great sales people, right? Research that analyzes successful sales people has demonstrated that the more the customer speaks, the more likely the customer is to buy. In many situations, the customer already has the knowledge and information required to realize the real benefit of purchasing a product or changing a habit. The role of the salesperson is to help them clearly and simply connect the dots in order to consciously realize that benefit. When an open-ended question is asked, the customer must bring the conversation that just took place to full consciousness of thought to answer the question. Full consciousness of thought is where real change takes place.

A statement of fact or brief core selling message that establishes context, followed by an open-ended question, is a simple and effective way to do this. The statement of fact consists of a simple fact that uncovers a specific problem, emphasizes the benefits of a specific product, or both.

While selling solar panels to help the customer save money on electricity, an example of the statement of fact plus open-ended question could be as follows:

"The climbing cost of electricity is a significant burden for many households within the Phoenix Valley. How do those increased electric rates impact your family?"

The benefit of using the statement of fact before the open-ended question is to direct the conversation in a way that highlights a problem that creates a selling opportunity. The problem is brought to full consciousness of thought for the customer. This is the first stage in helping the customer begin to connect the dots to a significant problem, which in turn, opens the customer's mind to relevant solutions.

Depending on the situation, a statement of fact, followed by an open-ended question, or a statement of fact + an abbreviated selling message, followed by an open-ended question, is the recommended way to start a selling discussion with **Empowered**

Selling. A core selling message added to the previous statement of fact could be:

"The climbing cost of electricity is a significant burden for many households within the Phoenix Valley. Optimal Solar cuts electricity bills by 75%, which is the most cost efficient energy plan in the state. How do your current increased electricity rates impact your family during the hottest summer months?"

The statement of fact + brief selling message + open-ended question initiates full consciousness of thought around both the problem and the potential solution for that problem. A follow-up question could be, *"What would saving most of that money going out on electricity mean to your family?"*

The statement of fact + open-ended question and the brief selling message + open-ended question can also be layered in approach, one after the other, as shown below.

"The climbing cost of electricity is a significant burden for many households within the Phoenix Valley. How do your current increased electricity rates impact your family during the hottest summer months?"

"Optimal Solar cuts electricity bills by 75%, which is the most cost efficient energy plan in the state. What would saving most of that money going out on electricity mean to your family?"

I find myself using the layered method most often. The layered approach allows the focus to be on first, just the problem, and second, just the solution to that validated customer problem.

A Statement of Fact + Open-Ended question can be used very effectively throughout the sales discussion and was used to summarize and trial close *(determine if the customer is willing to buy)* the example of selling a luxury car discussed previously.

In a situation where the customer is considered an expert in an area, like we see when a pharmaceutical salesperson is speaking to a rare-disease specialist about medications used to treat the condition, a slightly different approach is used to increase message impact. The core message is the same, but how that message is set up and the open-ended question at the end is different. Pay attention to the adaptation in approach in the following example:

"You are an expert in this disease. I have never medically treated a patient. You know more than I will ever know when it comes to treating patients with this rare disease. From my perspective, it seems like Product X should be used as the first medication because of the disease modifying properties it has demonstrated. Yet, with some experts it's not being used first. What am I missing?"

In this situation, despite the salesperson knowing the clinical data about the medications, he has never treated a patient. Using the statement of fact to acknowledge that fact up front, recognizes the physician as someone who is an expert and important to those impacted by this disease. This approach works to break down walls that may be in place when a salesperson tries to tell a physician expert what to do.

The core message is set up by stating, "from my perspective," which again breaks down the potential defensive reaction a physician may feel from a sales representative that acts like he knows more than the physician expert. The salesperson is basically saying, "I'm not saying it is right or wrong, but this is what I have been led to believe and why I believe this."

The open-ended question is framed in a way that is asking this physician his expert opinion to clarify the potential misunderstanding for the salesperson. At the same time, the open-ended question brings the core selling message to full consciousness of thought. The physician must think, "why would this not be true?" If the core sales message makes sense in the customer's mind, real change occurs. The customer realizes a potential gap in treatment or an opportunity to do more for these patients. If gaps do exist with the salesperson's rationale for using Product X first, then the salesperson moves into objection handling, discussed later in this chapter.

Let's now look at some non-traditional sales scenarios for using the statement of fact + open-ended question approach. In an office setting, with a goal of creating a family type atmosphere, an office manager may say to the receptionist, "*you have such an incredible smile this morning. Tell me about what has made your day so great.*"

The statement of fact compliments the receptionist's smile, which, by itself, increases personal connection and brings down the guard of our customer. This statement, in addition to the open-ended question, directs the conversation towards positive experiences, which improves the positive feeling, connection and culture in an office.

A husband can use this same approach with a goal of rekindling a connection that has begun to wane with his wife. The statement of fact and question may look like this:

"You take such great care of our family. I can't tell you how much I appreciate you for that. Tell me about your favorite memories with your family growing up and what meant the most to you during that time."

The statement of fact shows appreciation and acknowledges the efforts his wife makes for their family. The open-ended request continues this positive dialogue around remembering the best family times his wife experienced during her childhood. I have seen this approach break down the walls that we as couples sometimes place around ourselves and literally rekindle positive feelings towards one another.

A nurse may say to her patient, *"you have had quite a run of bad luck with your health lately. You have been incredibly strong through all of this. Tell me about what gives you so much strength?"* In this scenario, the nurse is trying to get the patient to remember what she is fighting for. The more the patient internalizes her "why," the more likely she is to overcome the health problems that have plagued her.

Trial Close

During a sales conversation, the customer constantly evaluates the relevancy of the conversation. One misunderstanding or confusing explanation of a benefit can move the target audience from full consciousness of thought to mental disengagement. The trial close is just a simple question that is placed within the selling message that allows the salesperson to determine if the message is resonating with the customer. A trial close comes after the salesperson has already uncovered the customer's goals or mission. The trial close is used to validate that we have successfully connected the features and benefits of our product, service or concept to the goals of our customer.

Let's look at an example of selling protein powder at a supplement shop. In this situation the salesperson uncovered that the customer's reason for visiting the supplement shop was to "bulk up and increase lean muscle mass." *"This specific protein not only increases the percent of protein available for muscle absorption, which reduces recovery time and rapidly promotes increased muscle mass, but this supplement also does this without the negative impact of increasing the bad cholesterol in your body, promoting better overall health. Are these the types of muscle growth and health related features that are important to you?"*

If the answer is *yes* to the specific trial close question, the sales process continues to further reinforce features and benefits important for that customer to know about the product, or, if everything that the customer needs to know has been satisfied, the salesperson simply closes the call and completes the sale.

Even when we think we know what is important to the customer, a trial close should be used to reaffirm that our understanding of what is important to that customer is correct and that we have explained the product's features and benefits in a way that resonates with our target audience. The trial close is usually a closed-ended question that requires a *yes* or *no* answer because it is used to just affirm what has already been uncovered and validates that we have successfully connected features and benefits of the product we are selling to meet the customer goals.

If what is important to the customer does not resonate with the current sales message, the sales discussion should be redirected towards what is. If the goals or mission had not already been uncovered, the closed-ended question would be replaced with an open-ended question. When the customer likes the features and benefits, but has a barrier to purchase, such as cost, the sales process pauses and moves into objection handling to determine if this is truly the right product for the customer. This is an opportunity to clarify or shed more light on the areas that the customer does not fully understand that may eliminate the barrier to buy.

Objection Handling

After the trial close in the supplement shop, let's assume that the customer did not give a clear answer. Instead, he asked, how much does this product cost? As the price is shared with the customer, his eyes get big and he takes a step back.

Noticing these non-verbal cues, the salesperson asks, *"Is that cost a concern for you?"*

"This is just more than I was anticipating spending on protein powder."

The stages of Objection Handling include: acknowledge, clarify, empathize, address, and confirm. The salesperson at the supplement shop may objection handle as follows:

Acknowledge: *"Cost is an important thing to consider when looking at purchasing supplements."*

Clarify: *"To clarify, your concern is around the value of this product and that it will end up costing a lot more money than a basic whey protein. Do I have that right?"*

Empathize: *"I get it, everything feels expensive these days and we have to pick and choose where we spend our money. The initial cost of this product also had me asking the same question."*

Address: *What personally sold me is the fact that you only take half the amount that you would take with a standard whey protein to get the same absorption to promote muscle growth. That means one container of this product is equivalent to two containers of basic whey protein. This product costs more up front, but costs less month over month. On top of that, this product reduces recovery time, allowing you to get more work in, which* *promotes rapid growth over a shorter period of time. If muscle growth is the goal, this product is the best value on the market."*

Confirm: *"Does that make you feel better about the initial cost?"*

Every person wants their concerns to be heard. Acknowledging a concern says to the other person, "I hear you."

What we hear as the objection is not always the real objection. Clarifying ensures that the salesperson discusses what is most relevant to the customer. Sales people in professional settings, as well as social settings, often elaborate extensively on areas that do not address the real concern. Clarifying prevents that.

Empathy is a step that is often missed, yet is very important to personally connect with the customer. Empathy demonstrates the fact that the salesperson truly understands and cares about the concern, again, going back to the old adage, "people don't care about what you know until they know that you care."

Addressing is where relevant and clarifying information is shared to help the customer better understand the product, service, features, and real benefits. As with the core selling message, objection handling should be boiled down to simple and specific features and benefits that are relevant to the discussion. Less is more. The more information that is shared that is irrelevant to the true concern, the more the relevant message is diluted.

Confirming ensures that the concern has been effectively addressed.

An important concept to remember while objection handling is to avoid telling your customer that they are wrong or to put them in a position to feel dumb for decisions they have made. What is the natural reaction for most people when we say or do something we perceive as stupid? We want to get away from the situation, right? Our customers feel the same way. Allow your customers to save face, even when they are wrong.

As a salesperson, take ownership for the misunderstanding. *"We have done a poor job highlighting the differences in these medications. It makes sense why you have been using the competition. The competition is a good drug."* Empathize with why someone in the customer's position would feel the way they do. *"I felt the exact same way as you do. I get it."* The fundamental concepts discussed during the personal connection portion are applicable here and throughout every stage of **Empowered** Selling.

Disagreements in a personal relationship follow the same process as they do in a professional setting. Consider the following discussion between a husband and wife, where the husband is concerned about his wife increasing her travel for work:

Husband's Objection:

"We can't take care of the needs of our family with you gone all the time."

Wife's Objection Handling:

Acknowledge: *"Being gone more is tough on the family. I realize that."*

Clarify: *"Are you most concerned about getting the kids to and from school and activities or our family time together?"*

Empathize: *"I understand. It's hard for me to even consider how we would take on everything that you do while you're here at home if your job required you to travel overnight."*

Address: *"I have spoken to my parents about coming out to help us for six months while my travel increases, which will help get the kids where they need to be. Not being in the home isn't ideal, but I would love to face-time with you and the kids each night to hear about your day and to share mine. This may not be easy, but by taking this travel rotation, I am in a better position to take a local promotion that pays more money and does not require the travel I have now in my current position. It's tough now, but things will be easier for us long-term if I take this opportunity."*

Confirm: *"Does this make you feel any better about potential temporary travel?"*

If we are aware of what the likely objection will be, a very effective way to proactively address the potential roadblock to buying is by simply and specifically stating the objection upfront with a statement of fact, followed by an open-ended question. The example of the supplement shop scenario could be framed like this:

"This protein supplement costs twice what the competing whey protein costs, but the value it brings is more than twice. This

protein supplement is the greatest value, if the goal is rapid lean-muscle growth. What are your primary goals for purchasing a protein supplement?"

As a penny pinching customer, instead of waiting for the ball to drop on cost, now I'm intrigued and fully engaged in assessing and analyzing what makes this protein supplement so special. How will the added features of this supplement benefit me and my goals?

The husband's objection to his wife traveling more for work could be framed as follows:

"I have just been offered a promotion that requires more travel, but it also offers what I believe is the best opportunity for us to have more time and less financial stress over the long run. How do you feel about 6 months of increased travel, if it meant $30,000 more a year and more time at home after this rotation is complete?"

As the husband, I'm not excited about hearing that my spouse may be gone more than she already is, but I am also now curious and fully engaged on how this opportunity will provide that increased financial and increased family time benefits over the long-run.

Close (the Call to Action)

A common "close" that sounds like fingernails on a chalkboard to me, and that I have found used frequently in the pharmaceutical industry is, "Will you CONSIDER product X for your patients?" After the physician answers *yes*, I have often sat and watched the physician's wheels in their mind turning in an internal dialogue that says, "yeah, I'll consider it. Already did, but I'm comfortable with the competition and I'm going to continue to use it." The sales representative walks out of the office satisfied with the sales call, yet the weeks following this sales interaction do not bring in any additional prescriptions.

The sales call close must be simple and very specific to the desired outcome. It is a call to action. In pharmaceutical sales, the desired outcome is not for the physician to CONSIDER using the product. The desired outcome is for the physician to PRESCRIBE the medication, resulting in better patient outcomes. A simple and specific close in the pharmaceutical market can include:

"There are no perfect medications, but for patients who are greater than 60 years old and who have high blood pressure, product X provides the only proven benefit. Will you use product X in those patients?"

In this close, exactly what is being asked is clear, simple and specific. A *yes* completes the sale. A *no* says there is more work to be done. When the sales call is complete, the pharmaceutical salesperson knows whether or not the interaction has been a success. There is no guessing when simple and specific closes are used.

The most impactful closes include a brief summary of the most relevant parts of the message *(only proven benefit)* and have a very specific call to action *(Will you use product X in patients greater than 60 years old with high blood pressure?).*

In the husband and wife example addressed in the objection handling section, a simple and specific close could be:

If my parents can come help, so that we are confident everything can be handled, I would like to make this sacrifice now for our future. I know this will be hard on all of us, but I will ensure that I set apart time each day to connect with each of you. Will you support this travel rotation?

Another angle for a close with each of the examples provided above that I often use in situations when I am speaking to an expert or an individual that a direct close doesn't resonate with is as follows: "*As you confirmed, only product X has demonstrated a clear benefit for patients greater than 60 years old. I realize there are other things to consider, but knowing that, what would be your hesitancy in primarily using product X in that population?*" "*You mentioned having 5 to 10 elderly patients with this condition. Is product X something you feel those patients should be on?*" "*What can I do to support you with the prescriptions for those patients?*"

For the husband and wife discussion on work travel, "*You agree that my parents coming here to help will make things more manageable and that if we set time apart each day to connect, it will help. I would like to make this sacrifice now for our future. Knowing that, what would be your hesitancy in supporting this travel rotation?" "What else can I do to support you and our family during this time?"*

The question, *"what would be your hesitancy..."* brings both the pros and cons of the discussion to full consciousness of thought. This helps to overcome the emotional response of just saying "no." The customer must consciously consider, "what is holding me back from doing this?" The answer does not necessarily need to come immediately. While watching the body language of my customer, I may say, *"don't answer now. Think about it. Your perspective on this is important to me. Do you mind if we talk about it more in a day or two?"*

The dialogue in the close summary is also slightly adapted by reminding the customer of what he or she said or confirmed. The customer's words, versus mine, are primarily used to help the customer connect the dots of the benefits they will receive. The customer is placed in a position where their words, opinion and decision are important and respected by the salesperson.

The statement and question, *"You mention having 5 to 10 elderly patients with this condition. Is product X something you feel those patients should be on?"* brings the desired action down to current specific patients, which increases the probability of action, as compared to just speaking about patient types. The physician must bring his current patients to full consciousness of thought and evaluate, "should these specific patients be on product X?"

The close is a natural progression of the sales call. I often see sales professionals deliver a tremendous opening, uncover the mission of the customer, handle objections effectively and then miss the close. The close brings the desired action to full consciousness of thought for the customer and moves the customer to action. Two identical sales interactions, except for the fact that one has a simple and specific close and the other does not, have very different probabilities on completing the sale. With **Empowered** Selling, you are not asking the customer to give you something. You are solidifying a mutually beneficial interaction.

Practical Application:

1. **Statement of Fact + Question:** Formulate and write down a statement of fact + open-ended question that directs a conversation towards an unmet need for someone in your social circle (e.g. family member or friend) and for an internal or external customer within your profession. Commit to doing this every day for seven days. Each day write down how this tactic directed the conversation. How did your customer respond verbally? How did your customer respond nonverbally? How did this approach impact creating win-win solutions for meeting an unmet need? How was your customer response to this approach different than in the past?

2. **Objection Handling:** Identify a personal or professional selling discussion that you are going to have that you anticipate your customer objecting to. What do you anticipate that objection to be? Write down how you will respond to that objection by using the five objection handling steps (Acknowledge, Clarify, Empathize, Address, Confirm). Execute this plan. Was the objection what you anticipated? How did your customer respond to this approach? If you could change how you addressed each of the objection handling steps, how would you change them? Did any objections occur during other selling discussions? How would you change what you said for each of the objection handling steps in these other selling situations? Take time to write down your answers to each of these questions.

3. **Core Selling Message:** Formulate a brief (simple & specific) selling statement that answers the question "why your product, service or concept" to a soundbite that is no longer than 30 seconds. How will this message resonate with customers? How can this be adapted to customers with different goals? Does this soundbite give the customer a compelling reason to listen? Does this soundbite include differentiating language that separates your product from alternatives for a specific customer goal? Try this message on a real personal or professional customer. What was their

response? After executing this message, and assessing the customer response, are there any changes you would make to this soundbite?

4. **Close (Call to Action):** Consider a personal or professional selling situation. What do you want to occur? Specifically, how will you verbalize the Call to Action for your customer? Write it down. During the sales call, adapt the language surrounding your close to relate to what is uncovered during your selling discussion that is most important to the customer.

<u>Summary: Chapter 4</u>

- The core selling message should be *Simple & Specific*, eliminating unnecessary verbiage that distracts from the core message. Give the audience what they need, nothing more.

- Each product or service should be framed around a core selling message that is verbalized in less than 30 seconds and that answers the question, "why this product, concept or service?"

- There are complex issues that may require a lot of dialogue and explanation, but in each situation, the *Simple & Specific* summary points should be a focus at the beginning and at the end of the conversation.

- Differentiating language like *only, best, highest, most, unmatched, and like no other* separates your core selling message from the competition.

- The more the customer speaks, the more you sell.

- A statement of fact followed by an open-ended question is an effective way to bring the unmet need and/or selling message to full consciousness of thought for the customer. Full consciousness of thought is where real change occurs.

- The trial close allows the salesperson to determine if the message is resonating with the customer and determines the specific direction the remainder of the sales call takes.

- The stages of Objection Handling include: acknowledge, clarify, empathize, address, and confirm.

- When objection handling, allow customers to save face. Avoid telling your customer that they are wrong. Avoid putting them in a position to feel dumb for decisions they have made.

- When you anticipate an objection, stating that objection upfront is an effective way to set the conversation in a direction that focuses on the product, service, or concept benefits.

- The sales call close must be simple and very specific to the desired outcome.

- The most impactful closes include a brief summary of the most relevant parts of the message and have a very specific call to action.

- Closing significantly increases your chance of gaining a sale, regardless of the customer's agreement during the sales discussion.

5

Smother

Reinforcing Benefits and Forming a Habit

$E=mcs^2$

∎∎∎

Reinforcement and support (smother) is what keeps a good thing going. Smothering is continuing to feed the habit and to ensure that the decision to buy a specific product or service is a great experience and fulfills the unmet need our customer was looking to fill. Reinforcement and support is necessary to obtain repeat business and to obtain a consistent change in habit.

When an existing and competing habit is in place, the need for support and reinforcement becomes even greater. Many of the decisions and actions we take every day have just become part of what we do. We don't need deliberate thought to act on a formed habit. These actions are comfortable and bring a consistent result.

The ideal time to establish long-term sales relationships and customer habits are before existing competing habits have been established. Consider many of the desirable and undesirable habits you have today. How many of these habits, thoughts and perceptions were originated during your developmental years as a child? The professions of counseling and therapy are largely in place to help us overcome the unhealthy habits, thoughts and perceptions formed during those years.

For physicians, long-term prescribing habits are formed when a physician goes through residency and fellowship, which is when the real application of practicing medicine occurs, immediately following their graduation from medical school. The medical practices learned during this time have a greater probability of standing the test of time than skills or habits learned at any other time in their medical career.

Tools and products used during a plumbing apprenticeship create comfort and familiarity that can last an entire career. Rigid pipe cutting tools and a Milwaukee Sawzall were the tools I was personally trained on as a teenager and young adult. At age 43, 25 years after my apprenticeship, these brands continue to be what I use for home improvement projects.

Creating win-win selling opportunities during this habit forming time in your target customer's life, career, or developmental stage, will increase long-term sales for a given product, lesson or concept, with less effort, than any other time.

With that said, ideal timing is not always possible. Children become adults. Physicians complete their residency and fellowship. Apprentice plumbers become journeymen. The adage declaring "you can't teach an old dog new tricks," is based on the fact that habits are tough to change once they become a part of our lives; however, it still happens every day. A more correct statement is, "you can teach an old dog new tricks, but only with strong and frequent support and reinforcement."

In the pharmaceutical business, writing a prescription for another medication requires additional knowledge around dosing, side-effects, and warnings and precautions that are often quite different from the medications a physician became intimately familiar with through her years of experience as a resident and fellow. With high stress, and as time becomes a depleting commodity, as is often common place within the medical community, "smothering," in order to change a habit, becomes even more important. The reward and relevancy to the physician's mission must be significant enough to warrant the work required to change. The greater the work required to change or create a habit, the greater the need for support and the reinforcement of benefits.

A dosing chart posted in the sample closet, extensive training for support staff, peer-to-peer meetings discussing medication nuances and adjustments required for different patient types, reinforcement of recent treatment success, an expert mentor, and frequent reminders of the benefits and actions required to effectively use the new medication are all examples of "smothering" within the medical sales community.

At home, posting a weekly job chart, dinner discussions on how the work completed positively impacted the household, and allowance directly tied to jobs done correctly are examples of "smothering" to solidify positive change in developing responsible children.

In the workplace, handwritten notes for an employee stepping outside his job description to provide greater value for a customer, public recognition of the positive actions performed, deliberate financial incentives, and the formulation of a mission or code of conduct that reinforces those actions and engrains them as part of the company culture is representative of "smothering" that takes place to continue and expand those desired actions.

Just as many married couples have discovered, a marriage will weaken without consistent reinforcement in strengthening the relationship. Examples of "smothering" for a husband and wife could include:

- Drinking coffee together to start the morning
- A deliberate note or text expressing love or support for something going on in your partner's life
- Genuine public compliments about your significant other
- Playful touch
- A night away without the kids
- Reading or praying together at night

Alcoholics Anonymous implements the "smothering" concept through weekly or daily group meetings, assigning a sponsor to check up on the recovering alcoholic, and a 12-step program to walk the individual through to sobriety.

The concept of *smother* is simple. Ensure that your customer has all of the tools required to implement the change effectively. The easier the salesperson makes the change for the customer, the more likely it is for the habit to result in a long-term habit. Existing habits often occur without conscious thought. Reminders and reinforcement are required to bring the implementation of the new habit to full consciousness of thought. Concepts of personal connection are also crucial during this stage of **Empowered** Selling. Personal connection creates loyalty and trust, which are very important for long-term sales relationships.

Practical Application:

1. **Smother:** Choose one selling opportunity you are currently working on. This could include creating a positive habit for a child, increasing personal connection with your significant other, improving the culture in the work place, or a professional sales opportunity. Consider the following:
   - What potential barriers are in the way of generating sales success with your specific customer?
   - What benefits do they receive by replacing any habits they currently have?
   - What type of support or reminders would make this change more deliberate or easy to implement?
   - What type of support system could be established to help with the change?

- o Personally, do they feel that they are important to you? What action can you take to demonstrate that you genuinely want what is best for them?

- Write down 3-5 actions you will take to support this change in habit over the next 4 weeks. Write down the frequency of each action.

- Schedule a time to check in with your customer at no more than weekly intervals. What is going great? What struggles is your customer encountering? Adapt the reinforcement and support appropriately with this customer specific feedback.

<u>Summary: Chapter 5</u>

- Smothering is continuing to feed the habit and to ensure that the decision to buy a specific product or service is a great experience and fulfills the unmet need our customer was looking to fill.

- Creating a habit requires strong reinforcement and support. Creating a new habit to replace an already established, but less desirable habit, requires a lot more.

- Targeting a customer when they are just beginning to develop new skills or habits in a specific area, as compared to changing already established habits, is much more efficient in creating long-term sales results.

- The greater the work required to change habits, the greater the customer benefit and customer support needs to be.

- The easier the salesperson makes the change for the customer, the more likely it is for the habit to result in a long-term habit.

- Personal connection generates trust and loyalty, which is another component important in smothering that results in long-term sales results.

6

Seize the Day!

Unleash Empowered Selling!

■■

In summary, **Empowered** Selling ($E=mcs^2$) components are simply explained as follows:

Mission: Internalizing and defining what you want to do and how you want to do it; defining how your product, service or concept improves the lives of others; determining the "why" that fuels your drive in accomplishing your mission when times get tough; uncovering the mission or goals your customers have.

Connection: Connecting how the features and benefits of your product, service or concept help your customer achieve their mission or goals; connecting on an interpersonal level; showing genuine interest in others; connecting on common interests

Simple & Specific: Giving the customer what they need to know in order to realize how the product, service or concept makes their lives better in a simple and specific way; helping the customer understand exactly what they need to do to gain that benefit

Smother: Engaging in activities that reinforce, remind, and support your customer's change in habit; making the change as easy as possible

Making the choice to develop any one of the **Empowered** Selling concepts of mission, connection, simple & specific or smother will literally improve your career, relationships, social interactions, and bring more fulfillment to parenthood. Systematically applying the entire $E=mcs^2$ formula will thrust you from being a spectator in the stands to being fulling engaged in the arena of life.

Just remembering the formula will allow you to walk through the components most important in creating mutually beneficial sales interactions. Ask yourself the following:

Mission (m):
- What is my mission?

- What is the product mission?
- What is the mission of my customer?

Connection (c):

- How am I going to connect personally with this customer?
- How am I going to connect the features and benefits of my product to the goals and mission of the customer?

Simple & Specific (s):

- Is my message and call to action simple and specific?

Smother (s):

- What support will I be providing my customer to make the change or product purchase easy?
- What actions will I follow-up with to ensure customer satisfaction, customer referrals, and repeat business?

Empowered Selling is not convincing a customer to buy a product, service, or concept. **Empowered** Selling is the act of helping others live a better life. It is the creation of win-win outcomes that transforms homes, communities and careers.

The life changing application of Empowered Selling does not stop here. Log onto Choose Your Fate world (https://cyfworld.com) for access to in-depth practical application workbooks that are tailored for specific personal, family and professional needs. Each workbook will dive deeper into practical application for each concept to help further your understanding, real world application, and mastery of each. Continue reading on to the appendices to see the selling process for scenarios discussed in this book from start to finish. Keep in mind, the exact dialogue is not important. What is important are the concepts ($E=mcs^2$), which should be integrated into your personality and individual strengths. Leverage the assets you have and embrace what makes you unique and truly you.

Carpe Diem!

APPENDIX

Door to Door Sales Call
Solar Power

Product Mission: To reduce the burden of high electricity costs within the Phoenix Valley in order to give the community more of their own money to do what fulfills them most.

Personal Connection: Finding something in common or of genuine interest to break down customer walls set up for salespeople.

Wow, your rose bushes are beautiful. Did you put them in yourself? My grandmother had rosebushes like that. I spent hours playing in her yard as child and can still remember the smell of them.

Statement of Fact + Open-Ended Question: Simple and specific information is used in the statement of fact and open-ended question to make the information shared more tangible to the customer. A trial close is used to validate that the information shared is relevant to this customer's situation before asking the related open-ended question.

Summer is right around the corner and the climbing cost of electricity is a significant burden for many households within the Phoenix Valley. Sun Valley Electric just announced a 4% increase in electricity costs over last year. On average electricity is costing homeowners $600 each month in June, July, and August. Is that similar to what it costs for electricity in your home? What would saving $1350 for just those three months mean to your family?

Customer Answer: *It would probably allow us to do a bit more with our grandkids.*

Statement of Fact + Open-Ended Question: Layered Statements of Fact + Open-Ended Questions are an effective way to set the direction of the discussion and to get the customer engaged and speaking.

A lot of people like to leave on vacation to escape the heat in the summer. Is that something you like to do? Where do you like to go?

Customer Response: *We like to escape to California with our grandkids when we can afford it.*

Statement of Fact + Open-Ended Question: A simple and specific statement of fact that uses information gained from the customer's answers to open-ended questions makes the discussion relevant to the customer. The Open-Ended Question brings the benefit to full consciousness of thought. The customer internalizes what is possible with the money that could be saved.

The money saved just during those three summer months will pay for 5 days at Disneyland for you, your wife and two grandchildren. The money saved would also pay for 4 nights at a hotel in California, plus tickets for two days at Six Flags Magic Mountain Resort or Knott's Berry Farm and 3 days at the beach. How do you feel your family would react to the news they were going on a trip like that this summer?

Brief Selling Message + Open-Ended Question: The message is simple and specific to the exact cost savings Optimal Solar provides, as well as the specific backing and testimonials provided by both the BBB and current customers. An open-ended trial close is used to assess if the messages and benefits shared are enough for the customer to commit to buy.

Optimal Solar cuts electricity bills by 75%, which is the most cost efficient energy plan in the state. We have a triple-A ratting with the Better Business Bureau and have hundreds of 5 star ratings from customers just in the Phoenix Valley. We have just installed solar panels in two houses in the neighborhood, Ed Jones over on Electra Lane and for the Johnson family on Elm Circle. How do you feel about getting solar panels installed to lock in a low rate for electricity and to start saving that money you can use for so many other things?

Customer Objection: *I can't take on the debt of installing solar panels, especially when I consider the fact that we might be moving to another community in a few years.*

Objection Handling: Acknowledge, Clarify, Empathize, Address, and Confirm.

Acknowledge: *It is very important to look at the total long-term cost of installing solar panels, especially when you may want to move within a few years.*

Clarify: *To clarify, you are concerned that if you sell your house, you will be responsible for the remainder of the cost of solar panels installed* *and you will not benefit from the cost savings it is supposed to provide. Do I have that right?*

Empathize: *I get it. It would make me sick to my stomach if after saving $10,000 on electricity, I was stuck with paying $15,000 to pay off the cost of the panels installed on my home.*

Address: *Many of the 5-star reviews have come from people that chose to sell their home just a few years after the initial installation. Optimal Solar transfers the service and contract to the buyer of your home with just a signature, making the transfer simple and easy for both you and the buyer. Realtors are also very educated in this process. The great news is that homes with the cost saving equipment of solar power sell for $10,000 to $20,000 more money than homes without it. Installing these solar panels with Optimal Solar saves you money now and will give you more money from the sale of your home in the future.*

Confirm: *Does that information help you to feel more comfortable with moving forward in getting an installation scheduled?*

Call to Action: Simple and specific summary of the benefits, a trial close to ensure nothing else is a concern to the customer, and sharing exactly what needs to be done to take care of his high electricity costs, results in an effective completion of the transaction.

With the amount that you can save each month on electricity, you will have the opportunity to do more with those grandchildren. If you choose to sell your home, solar power will increase the value of your home without a risk of being stuck paying off the equipment. Knowing that, do you have any hesitancy in moving forward with scheduling a date for installation?

This is the paperwork we need to complete. The first bill, which will be much lower than your current bill, will be due 30 days after the installation. What days work best for you to schedule the install?

Smother: Sending an article from *Consumer Reports* highlighting the financial and environmental benefits of Optimal Solar; sending a detailed report that analyzes prior energy use and the cost savings predicted with Optimal Solar panels installed; details around the ease of Optimal Solar contract transfer when homes are sold; a list of homes sold, the percent increase in selling price the solar panels added, and the number of contracts successfully transferred upon a real-estate sale within the Phoenix Valley; a reminder e-mail with the date and time of the scheduled installation with details around what that day will look like; a reminder phone call the day before the installation appointment; a follow-up call after the installation to ensure customer satisfaction; a follow-up call and survey after the first month's bill; asking for a positive review on Yelp and other consumer rating apps; offering cash incentives for referrals that result in a new Optimal Solar install and contract.

Door to Door Sales Call

Making Friends with Neighbors

Product Mission: To increase rapport, connection, and community support within the neighborhood we live in.

Personal Connection: Finding something in common or of genuine interest to start a positive interaction.

Wow, your rose bushes are beautiful. Did you put them in yourself? My grandmother had rosebushes like that. I spent hours playing in her yard as child and can still remember the smell of them. I live just two houses down and wanted to take the time to get to introduce myself.

Statement of Fact + Open-Ended Question: a qualifying question is used first in this scenario (Are you from Arizona?), which will determine what specific open-ended question is used. Follow up questions like, *tell me more about...* continues the conversation.

We moved here from Colorado about 6 months ago for my job at American Express. My husband works as a science teacher at the high school. Are you from Arizona? What brought you to this neighborhood? Tell me about what you and your family like to do for fun.

Brief Selling Message + Open-Ended Question:

We would really like to get to know you and the neighbors more to build a community that looks out for one another. Since you've been here awhile, what do you think is the best way to bring our community together, and for those of us that are new, to get to know the rest of the families living here?

Call to Action:

With what you mentioned, how do you feel about a barbeque at my house with just a few families to start? I've got next Saturday open. How does that work for you? I'll supply the meat. Will you bring a side dish? I look forward to seeing you and your family then!

Smother: Involves the customer in the process, which enhances ownership and engagement in the event; plans for follow-up activities that continues the mission of community connection.

"It was so great to meet you yesterday. So far, I've invited the Millers, Johnsons, and Steinbecks over for the BBQ. Is there anyone else you would like to invite? So far the plans are to meet at 4 PM, have drinks and appetizers. We'll start the grill at 5 PM. I've got some ideas for activities to help us get to know each other, but would love to get your thoughts as well.

Place of Business

Nutritional Supplement Shop

Product Mission: to improve lives by supporting better health and self-confidence with supplements that help people achieve their goals.

Personal Connection: eye contact; a warm smile; open body language

Good morning. I really like that necklace and cross pendant... I've been wanting to get something like that. Where did you get it?

Customer Goals/Mission:

What brings you into this store this morning? What are your goals for purchasing protein powder? What else are you trying to achieve? What has given you good results or even a lack of results in the past?

Brief Message + Trial Close: the anticipated price objection is stated up front to allow the customer to focus on the specific features and benefits for this product.

The price of this protein is more expensive than the other brands, but you only need half the amount of the protein with this supplement than you take with other brands to get the same muscle absorption to promote growth. That means one container of this product is equivalent to two containers of basic whey protein. This product costs more up front, but costs less month over month. On top of that, this product reduces recovery time, allowing you to get more work in, which promotes rapid growth over a shorter period of time. If muscle growth is the goal, this product is the best value on the market. Are these the types of features you are looking for in a protein supplement?

Call to Action:
I'll give you a 10% discount off your first purchase since this product is new to you. All that I ask is that you let me know how this product works for you as compared to what you've tried in the past. Would you like to get container today?

Smother: the platform for follow-up communication is established that will keep this customer coming into the store, ensure customer satisfaction, and result in future customer referrals.

To follow-up, can I get a phone number or e-mail to see how this product is working for you? I won't use your contact information for anything but ensuring that you are getting what you expect from this supplement. Customer service and support is important to me. I want to make sure that you are getting what you need to reach your goals. It has been a pleasure meeting you today.

At Home Sibling Sales Call
Positively Impact a Negative Attitude

Concept Mission: Help my brother see how a positive attitude can significantly improve performance and job satisfaction at work

Layered Statements of Fact + Open-ended Question: Gain initial insight. Use that insight in the tailored follow-up statement of fact and open-ended question that focuses on the positive (your mission).

You mentioned some frustrations at work earlier. Tell me more about that.

I had a similar experience where I started off in a rocky relationship with my boss after challenging something he wanted to implement. I thought it was going to be the end of my career there. The problem was that I loved what I did, and I liked a lot of the people there. Despite what's going on, you've been there for almost 3 years now. What has kept you from finding another job?

Brief Selling Message + Open-ended Question: The *Simple & Specific* statement of fact and open-ended question directs the conversation around what can be impacted.

What changed things for me was just being conscious about focusing on what I could change, what I loved about what I did and how I really liked the people I worked with. My boss had a control issue, but if I made things seem like his idea, I ended up getting most of what I wanted.

Changing my mindset from focusing on frustrations to appreciating what I loved and focusing on what I could do, changed not only my job satisfaction, but it also helped to shape the culture in our office. A lot of what you've mentioned really seems out of your control. What are some things you are able to impact there?

Personal Connection and Trial Close: The solution was not my idea. The solution was a lesson my brother taught me, which increases reception to the concept.

Part of what helped me come to realize what I needed to do in my career was thinking back on when you took me on your hunting trips. It didn't matter what happened, you always had another angle to try to get the shot you needed to bring home the wild game. If we were in the wrong spot, we moved, but I don't remember many trips that you didn't get the outcome you wanted when you felt we were in the right spot. It sounds like there is enough positive with your job that it is a place you want to be. Do you feel that the approach you used in the mountains could work here?

Call to Action: Accountability is increased with a commitment for specific follow-up.

I'm really curious to see how what you do impacts the culture. Will you let me know how changing your approach impacts your job and the culture? If there is something else you do that works, let me know. I want to try it.

Smother: Text at the beginning of the next workday expressing excitement to see how the new approach works; calling at the end of the work week to see how the positive attitude has impacted his job satisfaction and others he works with.

Selling to an Expert
Rare Disease Pharmaceutical

Mission: Make life worth living for patients through education by putting myself *in the shoes* of patients and their families.

Statement of Fact + Open-ended Question/Connection: Recognition of accomplishments increases personal connection.

I recently read your profile in US News and World Report. *Very few physicians are able to obtain a 5 star rating for the patient experience. Congratulations. That really says a lot about what you do. What do you feel you have done differently than other experts that has set you apart like that to patients?*

Brief Selling Message + Layered Open-ended Questions: Recognizes the customer as the expert, which breaks down walls and increases reception to the selling discussion.

You are an expert in this disease. I have never medically treated a patient. You know more than I will ever know when it comes to treating patients. I would love your perspective on a concept I'm struggling with. How important is corrective vascular remodeling in Disease X on patient outcomes and quality of life? From what I've read, the only medication demonstrating disease modifying properties like that is product X. Yet, with some experts it's not being used first. What am I missing?

Brief Selling Message + Trial Close: Rephrasing what was shared by the customer and interpreting that into a simple and specific message.

If I understand you correctly, there are populations that were excluded from the disease modifying trials, but the majority of patient types were included in the trial and those patients should be treated first with Product X. Is that correct?

Call to Action: The expert physician is solidifying her call to action with specific patient types. The salesperson is cementing it further by gaining permission to share that opinion, which further validates what was said.

What should I be sharing to those physicians not using Product X in those populations that were studied? Would you be okay if I shared your perspective with other physicians?

Smother: Share feedback and insight from other physicians you have shared the message with. Share this message with nurses and staff involved with these patients, which includes asking questions that uncover both successes and struggles they have had with the product. Supply resources that make the prescriptions easier for both the patients and all involved within the medical practice.

Objection Handling: What if very few prescriptions take place over the next month? There may be something else getting in the way that has been unaddressed. There has not been a verbal objection to prescribing Product X, but there is one through lack of action. As roadblocks or struggles with prescriptions, like insurance coverage, are uncovered, the

Objection Handling process takes place (acknowledge, clarify, empathize, address, confirm). Below illustrates how the real objection can be uncovered.

I've shared your insight with other physicians. Your perspective has helped them connect the dots on the additional benefit their patients with Disease X can have with Product X. Some are now initiating treatment. Others are sending those patients to you. How many new Disease X patients do you see in a month?

With what we had discussed, three out of four of those patients would be on Product X, but I have not seen prescriptions come through. What am I missing?

Selling to a Spouse
Blending Parenting Styles

Mission: Provide my children (and step-children) with the tools necessary to be happy, healthy and self-sufficient adults.

Goal: Align husband and wife parenting styles for the blended family

Statement of Fact + Open-ended Question:
Blending our family cultures and parenting styles has been tough. I believe, despite difficulties in uniting our family, the different strengths we have, and that each of our children have, can make us stronger and better than if we raised our children separately. How do you feel about discussing how we can be better aligned with our parenting to more effectively take advantage of our different strengths?

Connection: showing genuine interest in my significant other and what she has done well; uncovering similarities and areas that may be different that I admire and see value in

What has been most important to you to teach your children and why?

What have you done really well with your children? I see that as well. Tell me why you feel that way. How have you accomplished that?

I admire how comfortable and open your biological children are with you. I also admire the fact that they aren't afraid to have a voice. We know how they feel, which is important and healthy. You've done that

better than I have. With what you have expressed, I feel like we are fully aligned in the importance of God in our life and in the lives of our children. I believe that is probably the most important principle to come together on, and we have that.

Brief Message + Open-ended Question:

For me, I have had a strong focus on empowering my biological children to be self-sufficient so that they are prepared to be on their own when it comes time for them to leave our home. My biological children do their own laundry, they each have household and yard chores that they are expected to do every week. They only have a limited amount of time on electronics, which I believe encourages them to be creative and to work towards larger goals, like learning, expressing creativity, or practicing sports. Do you feel like there is value in those things? What specifically do you feel would add value to all of our children?

Statement of Fact + Open-ended Question:

It sounds like we both find a lot of value in what we have done differently. How do you feel we can best incorporate the strengths of each of our parenting styles?

Objection (mother's response):

Showing acts of service to our children, like cleaning their room when they're at school or folding laundry is how I show love. I don't want to lose that.

Objection Handling:

Acknowledge: *Being able to show love in our own way to our children is important.*

Clarify:

If I understand correctly, you are concerned that some of the activities I've mentioned incorporating with the children may take away from the way you show love and the fulfillment both you and the kids get from that. Am I hearing you right?

Empathize:

I understand. For me, the last thing that I want to lose is the time I spend in the mountains with my kids. That's how I show love. It brings depth to our relationship and adds fulfillment to our lives. It is important to be able to express love in a way that speaks to who we are. Do you feel like there is a way to teach independence, yet also allow the flexibility to perform acts of service?

Address:

From my perspective, we can have both personalized expressions of love and teach being self-sufficient. Both are very important. If our children understand that they are the ones responsible to have their chores and responsibilities completed every week, I feel that it highlights the love you show through acts of service even more. When you clean the room of a child or fold their laundry, you did it not because you had to. You did it because you love them and wanted to do something specifically for them.

Confirm:

How do you feel about that? Does that make you feel better about being able to blend both of our parenting styles to benefit our kids?

Call to Action:

From our discussion, it sounds like I can choose the battles more wisely with our kids to keep the lines of communication open. At the same time, setting expectations with our children about their responsibilities, while having the flexibility to show love through acts of service, is a way our family can benefit from both of our parenting styles. Do you agree with that? Will you help me as I navigate adjusting the way I communicate with the kids to keep those lines of communication open? When can we talk to the kids about expectations moving forward?

Smother: Talk each week as a couple to discuss, *How are we doing? What went well? What can we change to make it better?* Talk to the children about how the prior week went. Take time to acknowledge when each child embraces the change.

CYFworld

Choose Your Fate world

Choose Your Fate world is the unification of diverse people, diverse perspectives, and diverse strengths behind a common mission. The foundational principles are:

EMPOWERMENT

LEADERSHIP

PURPOSE

The mission is too spread Empowerment, Leadership and Purpose to those unsatisfied with their current situation and that have a desire to make a positive impact in the world around them.

Find out more at https://cyfworld.com

ABOUT THE AUTHOR

Travis N. Jensen has spent the majority of his career hiring, leading, developing, and coaching specialized sales professionals within the rare-disease and biopharmaceutical market. His teams have finished #1 worldwide for new product launch sales and have consistently maintained the highest national sales volume, while interacting with some of the most educated professionals in society. Travis has developed and facilitated corporate training programs, developed and proposed corporate strategies and concepts implemented nationwide, and has served as a consultant to both national and global marketing departments. Travis's professional experience and success expand beyond white-collar pharmaceutical sales to door-to-door vacuum sales, home mortgage sales, and change order sales within the construction industry, which occurred during his years as a Journeyman and Master Plumber. Travis has served as a mentor for individuals at all stages of life, ranging from interviewing skills for new high school graduates to leadership and career optimization for professionals with over 20 years of professional experience.

www.ingramcontent.com/pod-product-compliance
Lightning Source LLC
Chambersburg PA
CBHW070811280326
41934CB00012B/3152